Soulmade Love

K. R. Wes

Copyright © 2020 K. R. Wes

All rights reserved.

DEDICATION

This is not a work of fiction, nor is it a coincidence. These words come from fate. They are in her likeness which is as close as my words will ever be to perfect.

CONTENTS

2……….SPOTLIGHT
4……….PRESENT
5……….BREATHE
6……….SOUL EYES
7……….GOOD FEELING
8……….VIBE
9……….THIEF
10……..THE WORDS
11……..LAVENDER
12……..CONTRAST
13……..SPACE
14……..RESUME
15……..SOUL NAME
16……..ISN'T IT STRANGE?
17……..INK
18……..HONEY
19……..3:15
20……..PILLOWCASE POEM
21……..LITTLE LIONESS
22……..#IWGUIW
23……..LUCID
24……..CHOICES
25……..LINGER
26……..FEEL
27……..STORMY WEATHER
28……..JUNE 1, 2020
29……..WORKING HANDS
30……..BEST FRIEND
31……..CRAWL
32……..ART

CONTENTS

34.......DIMENSIONS
35.......MEMORY FOAM
36.......EXHALE
37.......NOTES
38.......PEACE
39.......FIRST KISS
40.......STARING PROBLEM
41.......HEAVEN
42.......GREATEST GAME
43.......WATER
44.......BY YOUR SIDE
45.......THE WORDS PART II
46.......HOPE
47.......VIBRATIONS
48.......BLACK INK QUEEN
49.......FIRST DATE
50.......CHALLENGER
51.......MAGIC
52.......THE TITLE
53.......LOUD
54.......TRIP
56.......R.I.P. OLD ME
57.......FRAMED
58.......SHOTGUN CONVO
59.......BELIEVER
60.......CURLY
61.......EYES
62.......UNCOVER
63.......MOMENTS
67.......SOULMADE LOVE

I saw magic once
In the form of a spotlight.
It led me to a star.
The curly ponytail swinging
on the back of your head.
It led me to you.

She told me the past is over
and the future can wait.
Be here with me.
Presently.

I saw you sitting there with an empty space
beside you that must have been meant for me.

Breathe.

Between the moment I saw you and the moment I sat down, I thought of at least a hundred ways to introduce myself.

Breathe.

If I had known then, that you were my lifelong and maybe long after, inamorata, this breathing thing wouldn't have been so arduous.

Keep Breathing.

You have eyes like soil.
"*I have eyes like dirt?*"
No, like soil. The soul of the Earth.

I really want to be right.
I don't want the false hope
The intuition.
The gut feeling.
I think you're the one.
I don't want to be wrong.

I love watching her vibe.
Sounds bouncing off the four walls of her room
And reverberating in the four chambers of my heart.
Beats that make us vibrate
In the sanctuary of each other's arms.
I love watching her spread comfortably in bed
But always leaving space for me to join.

We could set off alarms,
Alert the warden, and break all the rules.
The daring duo of you and I.
Your first crime:

Stealing my attention from everyone in the room.

I don't always have the words
To explain this feeling
That I'm feeling
About you.
They don't always come easy.
They are not always so profound and elegant.
Mostly, they don't rhyme.
If I could find the words
And add a photograph, a song, and scenery,
Then you may be able to understand the meaning
And feel all the feelings
Of the words:
I love you.

I want to write you poems of lavender.
Words that make you feel
Like shades of purple.

You cannot say it's all black and white
When she stands there breaking
Everything we know of contrast.

There is no space
Within me that lacks
Desire to love you.

You've been on repeat
For a while now.
Repeating romances.
Repeating heartbreaks.
Just to fill the space as if you're waiting
For the person to resume with.

When I lay my skin
Against yours, I can feel
The definition of serenity.
I wonder if that is
The name of your soul.

Strangers have told me
They loved me
Strange words coming from
Lovely people.
I did not believe them.
You told me you loved me
And I only questioned it
Because for the first time,
It didn't feel strange to hear.
How strange it is
To hear it and feel it for the first time.

Tattoo needle therapy.
Dig in to my insecurities
And remove my colorless vision.
I would like a portrait
On my atrium
Of you.
Heart on my heart.

You were never entirely my cup of tea.
You were the honey.
Sweet and bitter.
Bourbon honey in my chai
With a splash of whiskey.
My central piece of dulcet in afternoon tea.

Your cruising speed is 80
And mine is always 70.
Flying down the highway with your hand
On my knee feels like well over 90.

We sang about the time and how
You and I were on top of the world.

Every moment with you feels like
3:15 in a sand dune Jeep.

I've been trying to write all day.
The words were barricaded in my wrists
Until you came home to me.
From my fingers, caressing your cheek,
They flowed to the papers
Stuffed under pillowcases.

I imagine a smaller version of you.
Ferocious little lioness
Prowling in her mother's steps.

I watch her sing Kehlani
Like gospel
And I know she's the one
Before the chorus.

Butterfly wings tickle my throat
When I try to speak to you.
I stumble over simple words out loud.
It's here in these pages,
That they become lucid.
Dreams become reality and words
Make impressions.

She never had to try.
For her, it came easy.
The way I fell for her was like a spell.
I had no control.
But to continue loving and falling
for her over and over again was by choice.
A choice I would never stop making.

Linger a little longer.
Stay a while
And get comfortable.
Put up your feet
And rest your bones
From all the years
Of searching for me.
Linger with me.
You don't have to go
Or ever have to leave.
Linger in this moment
So that it will last a lifetime
And even far beyond.

"There's no way you've felt these words."

She placed my book on the counter
and smiled at me.

"How do you feel something so pure?"

I didn't know how to respond.
I thought to myself and wondered
how I would feel for someone like her.

Not every day with you is sunshine.
Sometimes it's a tornado
Of negative emotion
Tearing through our home.
Then, the eye of the storm
Falls upon us.
The calm within the chaos
As I look at the woman I love.
Despite the tornado,
We find ways to ride the storm with bed sheets.

"Hands up, don't shoot!"
"Hands up, don't shoot!"

The lights of the bridge illuminated your voice
as we made our way across.
With fists high and voices higher,
we stood together in solidarity.

For change.

I have never been the fighting type
but I have always been the type to stand.
Tear gas or rubber bullets, I continued to stand.

For you, I would take every hit.

I am not here to tear down walls.
I can build a window
And plant a tree beside it.
I can build a door and add other rooms
With furniture.
I am not here to disrupt your cozy.
I am here to give you more.

I had a best friend growing up.
From childhood to teenage years,
Best friends came and went.
Then you,
You stayed.

It's almost as if our souls
Are constantly trying to crawl out
And remove the space between them.

Art has no business
Being held captive by glass.
Just like you have no business
Being hidden in a tower.

"You're not even here with me right now."

I admit, I was spaced and traveling through alternate dimensions and timelines.
I am sure no version of me could be without you.

"I am always here, even when you think I'm not."

She has memory foam skin
I sink into her embrace.

We bounce to Jhene Aiko
and it's as if inhaling didn't exist.
We just exhale together and release.

Love songs bump
through speakers and chest cavities.
The bass rattles my bones
and every note is yours.

Sometimes, there is only quiet.
Arbitrary deep breaths
Filling the void.
Even in this apathetic peace,
I am so happy to be
Spending this piece
Of life with you.

"I really want to kiss you." I said softly.
She leaned in and closed her eyes

"So do it." she replied.

I thought I was dreaming as I stared at her lips. Those lips were waiting for me.

I stare at you a lot.
"What are you thinking about?"
You always ask as if the answer will be different.
"Hm? Uh... Poetry."
It's true.
I look at you and I think
Of all the poems I've read and written,
I can't find the combination of words
To describe you.

Pardon my stare.
I'm honestly just curious
How someone like me can be loved
By someone like you.
Am I dead?
Is this Heaven?

The toughest competition
Is always between us.
A test of who can love the hardest.
A game I will never tire of.

She dips her toes in the water
And she embodies it.
She becomes the waves, foam, and cloud vapors.
She is the downpour from my eyes
When she is no longer beside me.

I was never in the business of making you mine.
You will always be yours
And I will always be beside you.

If I could make a living with these words
So we never have to part,
I would write everything.
All the words from my heart.
If I could make a living with these words
So we never have to leave our bed
I would write everything.
All the words in my head.

Before I felt your love,
I worried if I was enough.
If my dark past would
Overshadow my future.
But then there was a small light.
Hope.
Hope that grew to trust.

I'm trying not to get repetitive.
Talking about how I love you
Over and over again.
But you are my favorite record
On an everlasting loop.
My ears crave your vibrations.

Black ink queen.
Black curls.
Black skin.
Black soul.
Black pen.
Spill on the pages
And tell me your story.

I walked past the window and saw you there.
My chest was tight and I tried to remember
Basic body functions.

When I walked through the front door, you smiled
And waved at me. I counted my steps.

3

Why did you choose me? Why do I feel like I may love you?

5

Just smile. Ask about her day and try not to stammer.

10

'*Hi.*" I think I've already started falling.

Every day I challenge myself
to love you more than yesterday.
To show you more than yesterday
and make every tomorrow
feel like our favorite days when we were children.

I have always believed in magic
And the power of the moonlight.
I met you and found power all around me.
In the sunlight, the water, and the ground
Beneath my feet.
I found magic in the way
I am loved by you.

You were a manifestation
From my poetry and longing.
I ran in to many blueprints of you.
Many who wanted to claim your title.
A title that would always be too heavy
For anyone except you.

I used to think about the future too much
According to people from my past.
You found me daydreaming and asked
About my thoughts.
I was almost afraid to tell you
but then you spoke again and said,

'Say everything out loud."

I have yet to regret it.

"Let's go on a trip."

I thought of where we could drive
and how fast we could get somewhere.
Maybe if we had the money for a
spontaneous plane ride.

"I don't have much to get us anywhere."

She held my face and stamped me with her smile.

"Who said anything about putting on pants?"

She called me patient.
She called me understanding.
She called me many things
That many others would disagree on.
She knows the parts of me they knew
And the parts that they never will.

Everything better than the old me.

It started on an air mattress.
The first blissful and rough night's sleep.
We built ourselves up on rickety frames
And unstable boards.
We have come so far
And we are only going further.

Who needs sleep when
The woman of your dreams
Is sitting in your passenger seat
At 2am talking about
Everything that comes to mind.

She doesn't even realize
I would move mountains for her,
Simply because she makes me believe I can.

Her hair curls like twine
Around my heart
When she lays her head on my chest.

She always asked if I was really looking at her. To be honest, it was hard not to gaze.

"No, I need you to see me. Not just me, right here."

"I... I don't understand."

"Just look."

She covered her face, leaving only her eyes and I finally saw her for the first time. Brown and beautiful. Pupils wide and searching. Searching for that connection.
I found her.

I see you.

I will read all the words
Beneath your cover.
I will uncover
The words
Beneath your soul

We were unknown to each other
Until we shared glances across
Pool tables.
Our eyes were the darts
Our souls threw on target.
So many moments
Of catching stares,
Standing too close,
And small touches.

So many moments
That I want to revisit over and over.
So many more
That I can't wait to experience.

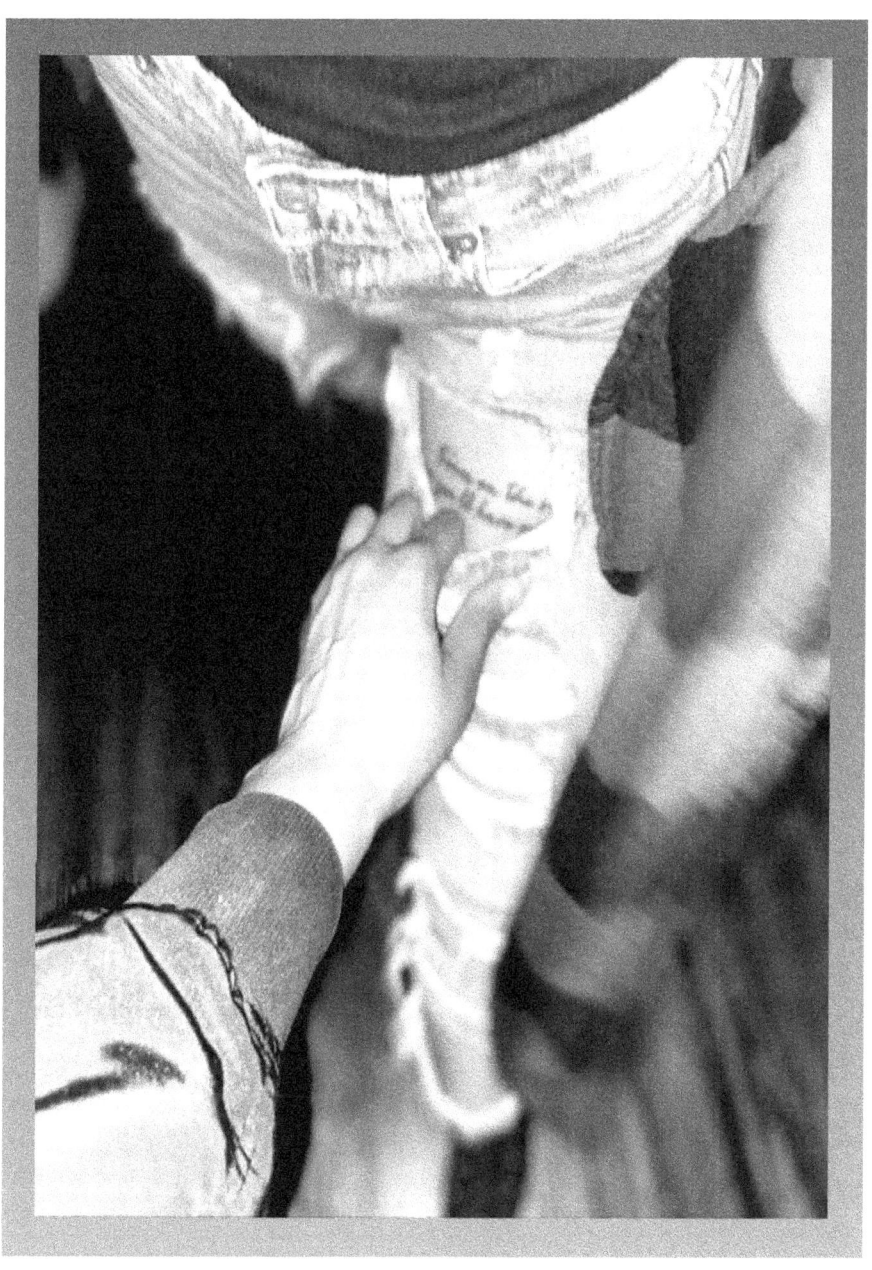

Photography: K. R. Wes
Model: Kendall Richardson

Acknowledgements

Dedicated to the most beautiful sunflower for consistently pushing me to be better and believing in me through every step of the way

Friends and family who have helped to keep my head above water. Without your support, this wouldn't be possible.

Soulmade Love

I put my hands to work.
I put my body and mind into words of love.
Through the motions and actions
Of my physical being, my soul was the master.
More than the simplicity of handmade,
I went with the complexity of soulmade.
My soul.
The source of my love for you.

www.ingramcontent.com/pod-product-compliance
Lightning Source LLC
Chambersburg PA
CBHW050918160426
43194CB00011B/2456